Oleander

modraji books

Oleander

Fiona Zerbst

Publication © Modjaji Books 2009
Text © Fiona Zerbst 2009

First published in 2009 by Modjaji Books CC
P O Box 385, Athlone, 7760, South Africa
modjaji.books@gmail.com
http://modjaji.book.co.za

ISBN 978-0-9802729-7-0

Book and cover design: Natascha Mostert
Lettering: Hannah Morris

Printed and bound by Harbec Packaging, Cape Town
Set in Palatino 11/13 pt

Thanks are due to the following people:

*Tanya Rojinsky, Carlos Miguel Fernandes
and my husband Omar Mustafa Hamed*

Contents

Remembering S-21, Cambodia

– for Vann Nath

I.
This was a school
before it was wire and silence.

Oleander
scented the sunlit courtyard.

This was a school,
with blackboards, white-

and-tan-tiled floors. Children
filled the concrete stairwells.

Then it was wire, shackles,
prisoners taken

from their families. They were beaten,

starved, herded like children,
helpless, fed a gruel

of watery rice. Obedient,
they still starved.

II.
Vann Nath, the painter,
drew his captor's head.

Kept alive on a whim,
he drew each line

8

like a precious, living thing.
Each line a lifeline

as long as his captor's
vanity saw likeness there.

III.
A worker told Vann Nath, 'Just let things be.'
'Death stays close to us,' he said. Vann Nath drew

and sculpted. Nothing else for him to do
but stay close to the enemy, keep silent.

IV.
Under the oleander,
in the silence,
it is a lovely garden.
Children must have

played here, enjoyed
the morning sunlight,
before their parents
fetched them; before dark.

Moths

At night, they bloom to light, like buds that burst
for air. As if they had no wings, they startle
into glass. That muffled knock
again, again, again –
they are like stars that break against the darkness,
break like vases,
brown containers,
tiny insect vessels of a great hope; longing
for the light; even dying for it.

Relics

Hold a broken bowl.
Touch a rotting comb.
History offers relics,
heavy, sacrificial.

Here's a man in bronze.
Here's a girl in stone.
On the flaking wall,
in the dusty well,

secrets that we guess at,
names we can't quite read.
Like a lonely ruin,
overgrown with weeds,

this is how life seems.
And we hold its best at
arm's length, afraid to say
we've broken into

tombs and found them empty . . .

Learning to box

After a year, I started throwing
punches in my sleep.
A left jab.
A right hook.

I didn't dream
of the ring, or fights.
I didn't see my opponents.

Fear and sweat
were far away, as they
are when finally
it is just me

with my footwork,
natural speed, the will to live.

And yet, in my sleep,
I began to throw
the kind of punches
boxers only

dream about.

Impermanence

Windblown, year-end nothingness.
Broken lines of Christmas trees.
Milky lake of sea from all
these windows. Lights now perilous
and faint through leaves
of palms. We pause,

observing as the stunned world grieves.

Asia coughs, half-drowns as two
tsunamis leave the beaches torn
with corpses, yellow buddhas, rings
and smashed-up history. Tiny wrecks.
Sun sets, as it always does: we
drown in unprotected sex.

Comfort

Rain's residual salt, its porous falling,
brought me to that moment, at my window,
when I saw the chalk of clouds break open,
loosening the tears in me, as if no
day could pass without my needing comfort.

How the wet earth seethed against a tree
vertical and blackened by the rain's long
strokes . . . how the river had no need of me
but let me add my few tears to the stream.
Just like a child who comes into a circle

holding out her hands, and finding new hands
not unwilling to allow a stranger
comfort. In the year of our divorce,
winter's rains were uttered with a guttural
grating in the drains, below my window,

where I sat and waited for my life.
Now the rain's magnanimous. Its wet hands
pat the sullen earth; its tiny drops
are pinpricks of my former pain. And wet salt
shivering on leaves is like an omen:

what was once alive; what can be again . . .

Red plum blossoms

Yao Shou,
The Master of Cinnabar Hill,
Is painting blossoms.

Red plum blossoms.

Yao Shou
Claps freezing hands
Together, dusts the snow

To read the canvas.
Dark red wells up suddenly
Out of the dazzling whiteness.

This is unsurprising.

Red plum blossoms
Sharpen his taste for art.

Hart Crane, 1899-1932

Prodigal, shucking off the first-class hell
of being you in bar and cheap hotel,
you leapt. The *S.S. Orizaba* churned
on anyway; propellers flensed and burned
the waters battering towards New York.
A fellow passenger, who saw you leap
and thrash, watched only for your body's cork
to float up. As she shudders into sleep,

the juddering vessel, droning, is the bell
that sounds your verses, amplifies your voice,
American Rimbaud. Given the choice,
would you have gulped the broken world as well
in sober hopelessness? Your sailor's voice
must first be lost in fatal tides to tell.

Shepherdess

'Think not, when woman's transient breath is fled,
That all her vanities at once are dead

. . .

Since painted, or not painted, all shall fade,
And she who scorns a man must die a maid'
— from 'The Rape of the Lock', Alexander Pope

In the room, your age set in.
Powder caked your wrinkled skin.

You were ugly, even then;
not a beauty, as you said.

You had the tired, shabby toughness
of an anonymous citizen.

So we rallied round you in
the weeks before you died; we came

to know the stale, unsubtle scents
of burning cigarettes; your silence.

Once, we cleaned your cupboards; I
unearthed a plaster shepherdess,

marbly blue and rosy-cheeked,
homely and grotesque.

I touched the little dimpled hands,
and the stumpy feet; the blonde

bun; the tiny, tilted chin.
You were quick to hover, anxious:

Don't drop it! – so you said.
And that hideous girl-ideal

plastered virgin who could kill
with a frozen, bow-lipped smile,

nestled there, against my palm –
slightly heavy, faintly cold –

petticoats not caked with mud;
sheep safe in the fold.

Death of a dog

'Lie down, dog. The fire is nearly dead.'

— *Ruth Miller, 'The Fire'*

Driving through these morning hills
here below the sleeping mountain

we can see it, weaving in
and out of darkness, through the trees.

When we brake, ahead, it falls
as if our stopping checked its motion

somehow; and its little strength
became our needle's quivering zero.

Mongrel bitch: her skull a cap;
her ribs a ruined architrave.

Eyes that pant with each new breath.
Every nerve unravelling.

Then we see the dark, defining
mark, the blood that seeps on through

the wound of every aftermath.
She must have hit a passing car.

As she tilts her bony head
sideways, just to look at us,

we are witness to the death
moving in her grinning jaw.

So we hunker down beside her,
watching, as the moon goes down,

and a yawning dark approaches –
like some shadow on a lawn –

moving; watching; moving in
this cold, clandestine dawn.

Beach-town revisited

It would be good, of course, to go again –
return to that salt hill, its dried-out beauty
shorn to black and tan; some lonely cry
quite clear; an airborne seagull's creamy wing
completing the unravelling of the sky.
And you, who took it in with tired eyes . . .

I focus on the hill, the bleaching sea,
that festival of grasses tinged with salt
like icing, very powdery, and stuck, dry,
to every living thing. (It burns the lips
the way a tear can burn them.) As you turn,
I sense the blur of me begin to burn,

to want you back, intolerably, trying
to think of some excuse, to sing some words . . .
A seagull perching on a ring of rocks
that waits until the wind permits a take-off . . .
I haven't any answers, but I offer
the best of me, aware of what's at stake.

It wasn't right for six years, but I'm calling
your name, the only name; and watch waves break.

July

July. The sodden grass. And leaves that cling,
resisting, to my boots. A solemn cry,
as doves, now settled in a palm tree's dry
enclosure, lose the will to chat or sing.
July. My eyes are sore. This light is wet
yet brassy, even smug, and minutes pass
the way a drop will slide across the glass:
too slowly, blindly. And I can't forget

July. The way it shimmers, glossy, damp,
like hair, or like a field of trodden grass.
I can't forget the things that cannot pass
before the eye, as shadows pass a lamp.
I can't forget the light, these flightless birds,
and all my dull, distraught and useless words.

Possibilities

The possible is
a room like the cell
of a monk. No dust.
A bed, a chair.

Anything happens.
Raw light reveals
the weave of a sheet.
A way of life

like walls, but not
restrictive. More
like visions, cool
and hopeful, where

a word is scrawled.
Or two words, three.
A monk is here,
just sitting here,

hands on his knees.
Outside, the crows
rake through
the black-hole-

black of trees.

Volcanic

Risk and aftershock,
this love
that leaps desire.

I cannot turn
my face from you,
so ash will spill

on lids –
residual tears –
and flame will kiss my mouth.

I cannot turn,
and this is good.
I know, now,

that the waters
boil below
volcanic ash, and fire

can never really burn
out, but attaches to
the deeper heat

around the mess
of colder ash.
Reminding me

this love, though dead,
is element;
and we, though rational,

are pure catastrophe.

Politics

India's alarming Pakistan.
America is rumbling, after oil
and vengeance. And I'm fumbling with one
completely dud, half-burnt mosquito coil.

It's winter. Still, those insects will attack.
Lights go out and houses in the street
begin to flicker. Candles offer heat
as much as arguments do, and looking back

it seems as if we've argued far too much.
The world's an angry red; the smudgy blue
of dawn-lit ash is arty, but the hue
is cold-cut bloodless; flesh you dare not touch.

We stutter with the paper's platitudes.
A drive into the country's dull and sad.
Not even death can end the bloody feuds
that families have and so I'm very glad

we don't have kids, my grandfather's dead
and nobody but you and I can suffer pain.
Last night, in a clumsy leap from bed,
I smeared a big mosquito as a stain,

against a wall. I wiped the dry remains
away this morning. Commas of our blood
were brown, unreadable. And later, floods
came swollen, breaking on a white-flat plain:

a natural disaster. Sheep and cows
went under, surging to a muddy end.
You held my hand. A multitude of 'nows'
came crowding back. Of course I won't pretend

you haven't stung me, gutted me, deprived
my life of air. I'm grateful all the same.
All's fair in love, war, etc. Your game
remains apolitical, hopelessly contrived

yet pure. The Middle East is poised for war.
Relief's been sent for victims of the flood.
Food and candles. Fresh-donated blood.
You reach me, wordless, as I cross the floor.

The dying fish

I'm drained of strength,
a fish too weak to thrash
for sea. On flattened sand,
I sense my end

in milky threads of seaweed,
or a scooping hand.
The air of me is clotting
to a drawstring line

and hook. My mouth's
hard bubble bloats against
the dryness of a rock.
No wave consults me

on shock or movement.
In the sun-warmed slime
of self, I am a paragon of need.
As patient as a leper,

watched and rotting.

Crime fiction

There's always a lake,
a body on ice,
a man alone.

Slab-cheeked policemen,
frigid women,
the silent phone.

Controlled addiction,
dictionary clues,
a cross-hatched bone,

a broken marriage.
foibles of life
lived out at home

where money's scarce,
children intrude,
peace is hard-won.

There's always the night,
a sequel to write,
a crime to condone.

I'm drawn to the scene,
a place I've been to:
innocence gone.

Butterflies

I.
On that shore
among the grasses, lilies,
fynbos, not too far
from sea, the salt-stung
spray of waves
and foam on bone-like
rocks, I saw
among the sand-strewn
pathways of the day's
demise, a sudden
rising up of blue-black,
almost purple, butterflies.

II.
It was more
like seeing nature panic
than unhand that stir
of wings, a beauty
much too strange
to hold. In salt-worn
shells, the core
of death lay hidden
but, like duty,
life, unbidden,
rose on flaky wings
to beat as living things.

III.

And I saw,
among the grasses, lilies,
soft, segmented wings
divide or shut;
amalgamate
with burning air;
wings, like hair,
that brushed my hand
and brought me back
to life. With death
all twisted round me then,
I took a shaky breath.

IV.

One can't ignore
the paradox of life-in-
death, a glass jar,
the net, a hopeless
ache to save
the thing that writhes on
rocks; the roar
of sea that shuttles
like a frenzied loom
and lies in wait for
us, for blue-black butterflies.
A foam sarcophagus.

North star

The garden brooded,
heavy with after-rain bruises.
With house-lights on,
I saw, through the pane,
a negative of some night-bird
on the outlined lawn.

In principle, these
epiphanies make me doubt
both vision and so much more:
I saw, as well, the north star
through the avocado
leaves; I saw a clearness

beyond that mass of leaves
and clouds, the verified
night-blindness of the night.
It was my self I saw,
as bright and true as mirror
is to mirror.

The guests were laughing,
tipsy with port's after-dinner
richness. In a tableau,
they seemed like chaos,
noise and not much more.
They dazzled each other, doubtless,

but I found myself staring
into the after-rain strangeness.
I fixed on that star
like a mariner, seeming
able to sail without compass,
future or fear, after all.

Reading Thom Gunn

I sat beside the open door.
Evening's thin, admitted light
was colder than it might have been.
I watched it sharpen on the floor

and try for lines of radiance.
But it was late, was far too late.
The lines in Gunn's *Collected Poems*
were fading even as I read

and only words of rational
and lustrous death stayed in my mind
as light gave up and bluntly fled.
Nor did I pause or hesitate

but pushed the book away from me.
Gunn is unbearably kind
about the affliction of the age,
about this age that is my time,

about a straining, unquiet mind
and Death's now visible head.

Wings

Angels have
the downy wings
of swans.

Of course, they're gold,
exceptional,
unruffled.

Just look at Fra
Angelico's
Annunciation.

Every feather
in its place.
Miraculous.

As women
comb their hair,
so angels fluff out

the silken
impositions
of their wings.

They don't complain.
They get around.
It pains them

to see we take
the sceptic's view
of things.

And Icarus?
He dreamt of heights
improbable.

A wobble
at that speed,
a searing fall,

was all he could
aspire to.
What a mad fool.

The angels laugh
to see men fly
at all.

Well, someone
has to suffer
some indignity

with wings.
They're always perfect,
very streamlined

in paintings.
You're a butterfly,
a swallow.

You can't lie
on your back. They're not
your playthings.

Angels dream
their downy wings
away.

They're dowdy
and unfashionable,
really.

But what would
ancient painters
think to say

to angels who
came hobbling by,
on sore feet,

to pass on
Divine messages,
or promises

of painless death,
of miracles,
of pregnancy?

The Temptation of St Anthony

'Outwitting hell
With human obviousness'
— W H Auden

I'm stretched out
in an altarpiece
by Grünewald.

Ice-white hills.
Shrivelled branches.
No escape

from this varnished
panel. Struck down,
as by sickness,

on my back,
and plucked and tugged at
with each breath.

In this altarpiece,
the demons:
my undoing.

Like a swarm of bees,
a pack of dogs,
attacking.

Don't look human.
Are one's demons
fashioned in

the oily hells
and feathered scales
of madness?

I can't stare
enough at claws
and beaks; the rough

and wooden staves.
Pox-wealed bodies,
glassy eyes

It seems that,
after all, they do
look human. They're

familiar. More
than dried-ice hills
of dreams,

or death-charred
beams of buildings
laid like trellises

across a landscape.
Choked with
fangs and antlers,

time itself
compresses
into foreground

and their stewing
brew of hatred
mocks me.

Far, avenging
angels come
too late. It's these,
my neighbours,
that I recognise.
I hold fast.

Welcome, demons.
Face to face.
At long last.

Leaving the summer-house

A muted field, where grass that looks like sorrel
tends to straggle; then a swerve of road
and spray of pebbles; then the sprawling house.

You've left it uninhabited and sagging,
for spiders and the filaments of dust and air
that seem to come alive. A crawling thing,

half-dark, disintegrates in movement where
the skirting meets a tufted curve of grass
that may just be a nest. The droppings of a mouse

attest to this. But did you stop to think
it might become part-owned by some dark, feral
entirely other animal? A half-wild thing

to prowl at the perimeter, its knotted fence?
Or did you think the world's defunct magnificence
could keep your house in order, dull, a planet

untroubled in its orbit? Here, beside the sea,
this house, the creaking world, your view of me
still rigid to a fault. But weeds have blown along

the taut ridge of the shore and seaweed flattens
against a glittering rock. This could be more
than just another landscape, yellow-staining grass

and love's corrupt enclosure. Let's drive out
on national roads again, towards a further town,
a crescent on some hillside. No-one can abide

an animal abandonment: and yet you've made
the house as plain, hospitable, as light arranges.
As we leave, the judgment falls to strangers.

Beyond

Let me fall asleep. Awake,
I pause before that inner door
and wonder what I listen for,
and how much is at stake.

Let me go to sleep. I take
the route of thorn and lavender,
of thistle, dew and fruitlessness,
of loveless words. I ache

for more than life can offer me.
The little stream, the sanctuary,
are not enough. I hunger for
the dreams that take me, more and more,

beyond that shut, that inner, door
beyond which is a lake.

Laguna Frias, Patagonia

Cold lake, you lie
in crescent peace,
as green as Venus
in the night.

My wide-hipped boat,
you barely roll
across a teasing
gauze of waves –

Hallucination
of this time
that freezes here,
a faceless clock.

And now a condor
veers to snow
above this planet,
cold, below,

and here I stand,
in bone-white air,
near water, reeds
and towers of rock.

Touch

Someone brushes up against you
on a crowded morning train.
Wool on wool – a warm arm finds
your hand, your elbow. Then he's gone.
What would you give – an extra hour
of travelling, dream-like, side by side,
in that winter crush – to feel
that touch, and to be warm inside?

On a lake in Patagonia

Gods and monsters
left these shores
as fabled as Ithaca's.

Tails of moss
and fists of rock,
the nebulous green

of constellations
in this water,
in these mirror-lakes.

And you glided
close to snow,
a diligent mariner,

legal, neutral,
making notes in
spiral-bound books.

Careful amateur,
mermaid-killer,
somehow not seeing

undergrowth's foot-
prints, tiny eggs,
an amber memory.

Convocation
of gulls and wavelets.
Chaplet of weeds.

A swill of darkness
within a shadow.
How to trace them,

delicate, hidden,
these living mythologies?
Eyes of green

and legs like splinters,
icy with age,
as bad-tempered Andes

touches the border
of Argentina,
this chafing jawbone.

Legacy – after Frida Kahlo

'We must sleep with open eyes, we must dream with our hands'
– *Octavio Paz*

I.
This column of air.
These nights of broken stone.
This flesh that speaks.

If Mexico is Frida,
It is also
Fig and prickly pear,

Water gods, dry ears
Of corn, torn as petticoats.

II.
Vanilla jar of dead water
Circled by a peacock.

This is what is left to those
Who linger in the courtyard.

Her legacy of nails in flesh,
Tears of pomegranate:

A broken column
Painted as herself.

III.
Frida dreams in turquoise;
Now vertical, her bed
A crushed infinity.

Reflected in her mirror,
This heart that frills the sand's
Dry life with blood.

IV.
This column of air,
These nights of broken stone,
This flesh that speaks.

If Mexico is Frida,
Then it is also
Paintbrush and suffering,

Icon of desire,
spine of jewelled bone.

V.
As she paints,
She dreams with her hands.

As we watch,
A butterfly sticks

To coils of her hair.
That flat plate of brow

Is a golden canvas
To feast from.

In praise of loss

Lose
Until the loss
Feels right.

Lose at cards.
Fold.
Refuse to play.

Don't respond
To provocations,
Words.

Don't invest.
Be certain
That it doesn't matter.

Hold yourself
Aloof; lose
The men you know

To other women.
Fold.
Refuse to play.

It's no shame
To spare your neck.
Let it in,

The knowledge
Of this loss
That is dying, living.

Fasting

You leak
like a raisin.

Mouth shut as purses
you lighten.

Organs shrink softly.

With sunset,
relief;

strange longing.

Burials

Plague time. Rags and crosses
dot the sand. Nobody wants to
cry above the sound of the now-dry
river, or the sough of wind.

Sand fans out around the morning.
Frail, tea-coloured fingers pick
at blankets. Two hands rub along
the beadwork nubs of spine, a woman

crying at this touch, as touch
is only pain. A dozen losses
knot up, like a weathered rope,
as grief builds in the throat again.

Plague time. Bones and crosses.
Burials. A dead bouquet.
Nobody wants to tell of this, or
hear of this. They want it to go away.

Shredding

My garden blooms
with naked, speckled guineafowl.
All pewter heads
and hunched-up, nervous plumpness,
they press into the green.
They tear my ferns
and stripes of shade, bamboo:
my swab of garden.
Autumn bleeds on through
in muddied water.

These birds peck
in sonorous chorus
as they scritch in mulch
and leaves; they duck, bob,
echo each other,
nervously spike their feathers
with redly carving beaks.
They shred the core
of what remains to shred.
They peck at my door, these
cockerels of the underworld.

Patterns

There is no peace
on earth.

Gravity makes its noise,
a factory hum;

the body's parts protest and shunt,
creak into life,
go on with will and blindness,
working cogs.

This poem
aches and chafes
for the belt to stop;

for lines and threads
to finger a pattern of birds
or flowers
on a rag of silk.

In Saigon

The war museum
was rather small;
I forget its official name.

It showed a handful of cranky tanks.

Men poked unmoving
propellers of aircraft.
A young girl touched
a gun's rusted nozzle.

It was humid. A one-legged man
sold books and begged.

It was all so sad

like a flower show
of dead blooms: brown heads
finally silent,

sent back to soil to fill
the darkening future's holes.

Light

Golden tiles
in golden flowers.

Now my eyes
are weary of this world.

In a little mosque
I found the light
once hidden from me,

tucked into the mind
of time and longing.

Golden tiles on gold walls,
Arabic the fabric.

All things aligned.

Beside the Nile

On the banks of the Nile
a city stoops,
city that never ceases to thirst
for its own inner light;
city beaten to pale gold under silver;
and the Nile
flows through my hand
and comes to land here...

On a hot night in spring,
through the flow and hum of cars,
the city's guttural murmur
is an undertone

much like a prayer sent out
among some chairs and tables
as waiters offer coffee
served in chipped cups...

On a hot night in spring,
there was nothing to regret,
and finally nothing left
but the evening prayer...

I sing to the Nile,
its lap-lap at its own sides,
its mute feluccas,
cool, cerebral breezes...

and while I remember
women crossing
with strings of lotus flowers
in their palms,
I see you still, oh Nile,

beyond the sales talk –
arch papyrus merchants
in their cheap shops –

I hold out my hand
and here you are,
Nile that watches the watcher
look at the water;
Nile that knows
a hundred crimes, excuses…

Wait for me
in a century of arches.
When I return to pray,
you will know my features.